CUT & COLLAGE

National Parks

*Beautiful Images of
America's Natural Wonders*

EARTH AWARE

INTRODUCTION

Collage, from the French *coller*, meaning "to glue" or "to stick together," is an art form with endless possibilities that dates back as early as 200 BC. A collage is created by piecing together different overlapping materials, such as photographs or paper, to create something new. Collage is a tactile art form, where the act of cutting and arranging materials becomes a meditative practice—a unique blend of textures, colors, and shapes that captivates the senses.

Filled with hundreds of vibrant, eye-catching images ready to be cut out, this book is your trusty companion for collage art. *Cut & Collage National Parks* invites you to piece together your own creations inspired by the surreal beauty of America's national parks.

The stunning images in this book offer inspiration for all your crafting projects, from collages and vision boards to scrapbooks, handmade cards, and school projects. Let your imagination roam free as you bring America's most beloved natural treasures to life. Immerse yourself in vibrant colors, intricate textures, and breathtaking vistas as you mix and match photographs, illustrations, and quotes. Featuring spectacular imagery of forests, mountains, water, deserts, flora, fauna, and outdoor activities, the pages ahead capture the diverse beauty and immense possibilities to be found in nature. From the towering cliffs of Yosemite to the otherworldly geysers of Yellowstone, each image showcases the diverse and unparalleled beauty of these iconic parks.

As you delve in, keep in mind that collage art is a wonderfully liberating process because it allows for boundless creativity and interpretation. There is no right or wrong way to create a collage. Let yourself be inspired, find what works for you, and remember to have fun in the process.

HERE ARE SOME IDEAS TO HELP YOU GET STARTED:

CHOOSE A THEME

You can choose a specific national park or natural element that inspires you to focus your collage around. It could be the grandeur of Yellowstone's geysers, the tranquility of a waterfall in the forest, or the majestic black bear.

EXPERIMENT WITH COMPOSITION

Play with different arrangements of your materials. Try a few different placements before gluing. Cut shapes, tear edges, and layer pieces over one another to create depth and visual interest.

TELL A STORY

Use collage to convey a narrative or evoke a specific mood. Consider how colors, textures, and spatial relationships can communicate the feeling of being immersed in nature's beauty.

CRAFT A VISION BOARD

A vision board is a collection of images and words that embody your goals and inspire you to reach them. Think on the person that you'd like to become, your short and long-term goals, and the places you'd like to visit one day. Express these ideals, emotions, and hopes in your vision board.

CREATE A MOSAIC COLLAGE

You can make a mosaic collage by assembling small cut-outs in various colors into a larger image or pattern of your choosing, such as a flower, tree, or even a person. Collect cut-outs in the colors needed and piece them together to create your vision.

EXPLORE MIXED MEDIA

Don't limit yourself! While you have everything you need in this book, you may want to gather additional inspirational materials to add to your artwork. You can incorporate personal ephemera, fabrics, magazine clippings, and even three-dimensional objects like pressed flowers and leaves to add a tactile dimension to your art and evoke the essence of nature.

EMBRACE SPONTANEITY

Lastly, you can absolutely go in with no specific vision or process in mind. Flip through the pages in this book and find what images you're drawn to, cut them out, and let your creativity guide the way.

As you channel your inner artist and cut, layer, and arrange elements to build your own unique creations, you'll find yourself connecting with the beauty of nature in a uniquely personal way. Whether you're drawn to the dramatic vistas of the Grand Canyon or the lush meadows of the Great Smoky Mountains, there's something for every explorer within these pages. So grab your scissors, unleash your creativity, and get ready to lose yourself in the art of collage.

LET'S
ESCAPE
TO THE
Woods

SEQUOIA
NATIONAL PARK

HIKING
HIKING
HIKING

BORN to be WILD

ADVENTURE

never
STOP
EXPLORING

wander

Let's wander WHERE THE Wi-fi is weak

OLD FAITHFUL GEYSER

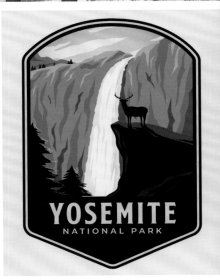

YOSEMITE
NATIONAL PARK

BEAUTIFUL
THINGS
DON'T ASK FOR
ATTENTION

Explore MORE

TAKE A WALK TO THE WILD SIDE

OVER THE
Mountains
AND THROUGH THE
WOODS

NOT ALL WHO *wander* ARE *Lost*

FIND
YOUR
SELF

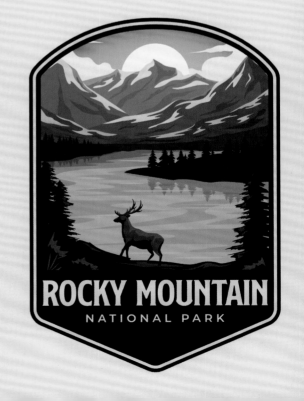

ROCKY MOUNTAIN
NATIONAL PARK

AND SO THE ADVENTURE BEGINS

IF YOU CAN DREAM IT,
"YOU CAN DO IT"

all
SUNSHINE
makes a
DESERT

ADVENTURE IS WAITING

keep
NATURE
wild

EAT SLEEP
Adventure
· REPEAT ·

FIND YOUR WILD

GRAND CANYON
NATIONAL PARK

ARCHES
NATIONAL PARK

MountainS
— are my —
happy place

GREAT
MOKY MOUNTAINS
NATIONAL PARK

MOUNT RAINIER
NATIONAL PARK

the Mountains
are Calling and
I MUST GO

keep NATURE wild

GLACIER
NATIONAL PARK

time
to Stop
AND
SMELL
THE
Flowers

SAY *yes* *to new* ADVENTURES

live life
in full
bloom

JOSHUA TREE

NATIONAL PARK

THE
WORLD
is →
YOURS TO
EXPLORE

STEP inside NATURE

Explore
MORE

Be
Adventurous

Free Spirit

I PROMISE **TO STAY** WILD

Wanderlust

All good things are Wild & Free

Never STOP Exploring

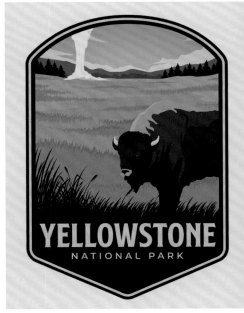

YELLOWSTONE
NATIONAL PARK

Merge
with
Nature

wander

MORE →

ENTERING

BADLANDS

NATIONAL PARK

NATIONAL PARK SERVICE

adventure is calling

ZION
NATIONAL PARK

GO WHERE
you feel
MOST ALIVE

THE WORLD is → YOURS

ACADIA
NATIONAL PARK

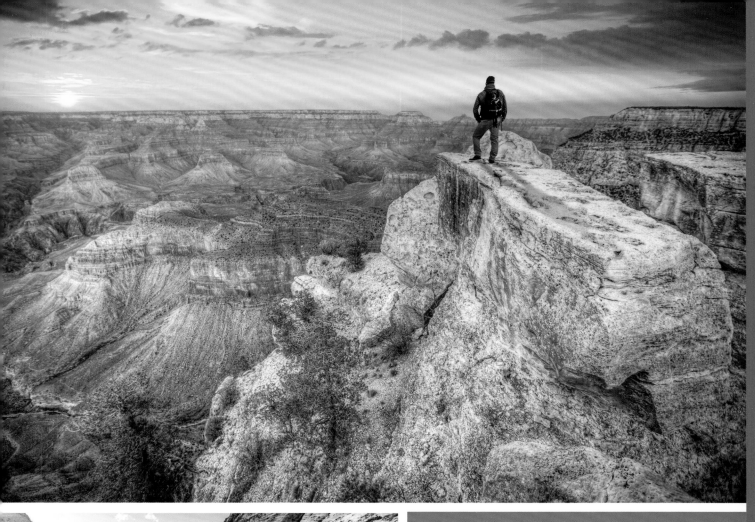

EXPLORE the *unseen*

let the
ADVENTURE
begin

YELLOWSTONE
NATIONAL
PARK

NATIONAL
PARK
SERVICE

EXPLORE
MORE

EARTH AWARE

An Imprint of MandalaEarth
PO Box 3088
San Rafael, CA 94912
www.MandalaEarth.com

Find us on Facebook: www.facebook.com/MandalaEarth

Publisher Raoul Goff
Associate Publisher Roger Shaw
Editor Peter Adrian Behravesh
Assistant Editor Amanda Nelson
VP, Creative Director Chrissy Kwasnik
Art Director Allister Fein
VP Manufacturing Alix Nicholaeff
Production Associate Tiffani Patterson
Sr Production Manager, Subsidiary Rights Lina s Palma-Temena

Cover design by Faceout Studio, Molly von Borstel

ISBN: 979-8-88762-138-8

Manufactured in China by Insight Editions
10 9 8 7 6 5 4 3 2 1

ROOTS of PEACE REPLANTED PAPER

Insight Editions, in association with Roots of Peace, will plant two trees for each tree used in the manufacturing of this book. Roots of Peace is an internationally renowned humanitarian organization dedicated to eradicating land mines worldwide and converting war-torn lands into productive farms and wildlife habitats. Roots of Peace will plant two million fruit and nut trees in Afghanistan and provide farmers there with the skills and support necessary for sustainable land use.

FSC
www.fsc.org
MIX
Paper | Supporting responsible forestry
FSC® C188448